BLESS THE BEASTS

CHILDREN'S PRAYERS
AND POEMS
ABOUT ANIMALS

Collected by JUNE COTNER

Illustrated by KRIS WALDHERR

SEASTAR BOOKS
NEW YORK

For my assistants, Cheryl Edmonson and Rebecca Pirtle, who do many great things to help improve my books; and for my four-legged assistants—Mary, our golden retriever; Allante, our black lab; Kiki, our frisky cat; and Mr. Tabby, the boss of the house— who all bring me endless hours of joy! —J. C.

For Colton and Daisy —K.W.

The author would like to extend special thanks to the following people who helped make this book as special as it is: Gemma Arcangel, Meghan Dietsche, Cheryl Edmonson, Christa Edmonson, Laura Eichenberger, Linda Eichenberger, Sam Eichenberger, Sharon Hudnell, Betty Isgar, Carol-Leah Isgar, Tyler Isgar, Michelle Kuhonta, Chelsea Lye, Denise Marcil, Benjamin Pirtle, Rebecca Pirtle, Margie Cotner Potts, Andrea Spooner, Elyse Trevors, Ryan Trevors, Barbara Younger, and Laura Younger.

The illustrator would like to thank the following people for their assistance with this book: Odylle Beder, Sadé Council, Colton and Jennifer Johnson, Daisy and Suzy Miller-Fuentes, Lauraine Anne Pell, Jacque Moon Yee, and Karen Zuegner.

Compilation © 2002 by June Cotner Graves
Illustrations © 2002 by Kris Waldherr
A complete list of acknowledgments appears on page 5.

SEASTAR BOOKS
A division of NORTH-SOUTH BOOKS INC.

First published in the United States in 2002 by SeaStar Books, a division of North-South Books Inc., New York. Published simultaneously in Canada by North-South Books, an imprint of Nord-Süd Verlag AG, Gossau Zürich, Switzerland.

Library of Congress Cataloging-in-Publication Data is available.
The artwork for this book was prepared by using watercolor, gouache, and pencil.
Book design by April Ward

ISBN 1-58717-176-7 (reinforced trade edition)
1 3 5 7 9 RTE 10 8 6 4 2

Printed in Singapore

For more information about our books, and the authors and artists who create them, visit our web site: www.northsouth.com

Table of Contents

A Note about This Book

Children are naturally curious about the creatures that share this world. Whether a tiny bug or an immense and awe-inspiring whale, they are drawn to learn more about them. I have often been delighted by watching little ones mimic the animals they love—how I admire their keen observations and their natural empathy! As a family of animal lovers, we have taken in many a stray pet over the years, and some even live with us still. Many of my children's fondest memories are of the pets that shared their journey from child to young adult.

Interaction with animals can offer much more than fun and companionship. Love of animals fosters a respect for creation and, indeed, of humanity. It provides a unique opportunity for the formation of compassionate values. Reflection about animals—about their place in nature and their place in our lives—can act as a door to a child's spiritual life and growth. And so, a unique children's book praising animals—one with a spiritual focus—seems an ideal meeting of themes.

Here you'll find poems and prayers about caterpillars, pigs, fish, frogs, horses, whales, birds, dogs, cats, rabbits, and so many others—whether in the form of blessings, profound or humorous observations, or pleas for protection. You'll find old-time favorites, such as "All Things Bright and Beautiful," as well as some of our most beloved poets, such as Robert Louis Stevenson and Rudyard Kipling. The included work of newer poets presents fresh views on the many connections between God's creatures and faith in our daily lives. And the children's pieces are written from the heart; eight-year-old Samantha Jorgensen, for example, expresses wisdom beyond her years in "Everybody Has a Heart."

Young or old, living or not, each author's insights prove that praying, or reflecting thoughtfully on the world around us, need not be boring or difficult. In fact, it can be fun. Deena Rae McClure finds joy in everyday chores in "Barnyard Praise," Carl Sandburg revels in the beauty of birdsongs and the miracle of life in "Look at Six Eggs," and Jacque Hall celebrates a pet in "My Best Friend." Many selections highlight how animals can teach children (and adults!) some of life's most important lessons: Tim Myers's "Child Watching a Turtle" shows that "strange" is a matter of point of view, and "Be Like a Bird" by Victor Hugo underlines the reassurance of faith.

It is my great hope that *Bless the Beasts* will inspire and nurture every child's innate sense of compassion and sensitivity toward the animals— and the people—around them.

June Cotner

Grateful acknowledgment is made to the authors and publishers for the use of the following material. Every effort has been made to contact original sources. If notified, the publishers will be pleased to rectify an omission in future editions. • Boyds Mills Press, Inc. for "Dragonfly" from *Lemonade Sun and Other Summer Poems* by Rebecca Kai Dotlich, published by Wordsong/Boyds Mills Press, Inc. Text copyright ©1998 by Rebecca Kai Dotlich. Reprinted by permission of Boyds Mills Press, Inc. • Curtis Brown Ltd. for "Grandpa Bear's Lullaby" from *Dragon Night and Other Lullabies*. Copyright ©1980 by Jane Yolen. Reprinted by permission of Curtis Brown Ltd. • Barbara Davis-Pyles for "Morning Song." • Maureen Tolman Flannery for "Angora Rabbit." • Jacque Hall for "My Best Friend." • Harcourt, Inc. for "Look at Six Eggs," an excerpt from "Prairie" in *Cornhuskers* by Carl Sandburg. Copyright © 1918 by Holt, Rinehart and Winston, renewed in 1946 by Carl Sandburg. Reprinted by permission of Harcourt, Inc. • Katie Heizenrader for "A Cloud of Fur." • Sharon Hudnell for "Pigs in Bliss" and "Prayer for Our Stray Kitten." • Samantha Jorgensen for "Everybody Has a Heart." • Susan A. Krauser for "Touch Me." • Arlene Gay Levine for "Once Upon a Caterpillar." • Sandra E. McBride for "For Flying Things." • Deena Rae McClure for "Barnyard Praise." • Dodie Messer Meeks for "Frogs." • Rhena Schweitzer Miller for "Bless All Living Things" by Albert Schweitzer. Reprinted by kind permission of Rhena Schweitzer Miller. • Laura E. Moore for "A Pet's Parting Prayer." • Cheryl Morikawa for "Please Help My Hamster Sleep Tonight." • Carol Murray for "Miracle" and "Reptile Smiles." • Tim Myers for "Child Watching a Turtle." • Shirley Nelson for "Bless the Beasts." • Marian Reiner for "Prayer for Earth" from *Flights of Fancy* (McElderry Books) by Myra Cohn Livingston. This poem first appeared in *The Big Book for Our Planet*, copyright ©1993 by Myra Cohn Livingston. Reprinted by permission of Marian Reiner. • Kate Robinson for "A Good-bye Prayer." • Hilda Lachney Sanderson for "Little Dog." • Nicholas Stephen Spanoudis for "If I Were a Blue Whale." • Patricia Lynn Spears for "Rejoicing." • Paula Timpson for "Horses Dance." • Viking Penguin for "The Prayer of the Little Bird" from *Prayers from the Ark* by Carmen Bernos de Gasztold, translated by Rumer Godden. Copyright © 1962, renewed in 1990 by Rumer Godden. Original copyright © 1947, © 1955 by Editions du Cloitre. Reprinted by permission of Viking Penguin, a division of Penguin Putnam Inc. • Donna Wahlert for "The Mother Goose Prayer." • Betty Williamson for "The New Kittens." • Barbara Younger for "A Dog's Prayer," "A Prayer for My Sick Pet," and "In the Name of St. Francis." *Permissions compiled by Rebecca Pirtle*

Hello, Animals!

PRAYERS AND POEMS OF DISCOVERY

All things bright and beautiful

All things bright and beautiful,
All creatures great and small,
All things wise and wonderful,
The Lord God made them all.

Each little flower that opens,
Each little bird that sings,
He made their flowing colors,
He made their tiny wings.

He gave us eyes to see them,
And lips that we might tell,
How great is God Almighty,
Who has made all things well.

Cecil Frances Alexander
(1818–1895)

Child watching a turtle

He's not the same as me.
He's short, and slow, and beaked.
He's wrinkly-necked, and stubby-legged,
and doesn't even squeak.

What would it be like
to carry every minute
that heavy, patterned shell,
to swim and sleep within it?

And yet if you asked him,
I bet he'd say I'm odd:
to him I'm huge and tall and loud,
too fast, too soft, too broad.

But here we are, the two of us,
alive in sun or rain,
and the Somebody who made us
doesn't think we're strange.

Tim Myers

Hurt no living thing

Hurt no living thing;
   Ladybird, nor butterfly,
Nor moth with dusty wing,
   Nor cricket chirping cheerily;
Nor grasshopper so light of leap,
   Nor dancing gnat, nor beetle fat,
Nor harmless worms that creep.

Christina Rossetti
(1830–1894)

A cloud of fur

How can a cloud of fur
Be such a comfort when you are down?
No one knows for sure.

Maybe it's his soft, light fur,
His triangle nose,
His pleasant purr.
Possibly his pink, bean toes?

But as I said, no one knows.

He waltzes through our house,
Brushing past us as he goes.
He makes himself happy on somebody's lap
And curls up for a doze.

A cat is more than a cloud of fur,
And he has feelings just like me.
A cat can make our home quite happy;
He is much more than a fluff to me!

Katie Heizenrader
Age 12

Miracle

The caterpillar's friendly,
won't cause you any harm.
He'll tickle through your fingers
and crawl right up your arm.

At times, it seems he's magic,
this fuzzy little guy,
for soon he'll be,
as you will see,
a lovely butterfly.

Carol Murray

The cow

The friendly cow all red and white,
　　I love with all my heart;
She gives me cream with all her might,
　　To eat with apple tart.

She wanders lowing here and there,
　　And yet she cannot stray,
All in the pleasant open air,
　　The pleasant light of day;

And blown by all the winds that pass
　　And wet with all the showers,
She walks among the meadow grass
　　And eats the meadow flowers.

Robert Louis Stevenson
(1850–1894)

Barnyard praise

I thank you God for morning sun
To say this bright day has begun.

I climb from bed, get dressed and pray
Then to the barn I make my way.

Cows at the manger, ready to eat,
They wait and dream for corn so sweet.

The sheep are noisy. *"Baa!"* they say,
And so I toss them their breakfast hay.

From up above in the big haymow,
I hear kitties cry: *"Meow! Meow!"*

As I put cat food into their pans,
They gratefully purr and rub my hands.

The rooster crows, the hens *"Cluck! Cluck!"*
It's time to go to the chicken hut.

I scatter cracked corn
    onto the ground.
And I pick up a basket—
    there are eggs to be found!

After giving them water, it's time to go play.
So I say with a wave, "Have a good day!"

But just as I start up a good game of ball,
"Breakfast is waiting!" I hear my mom call.

Inside at the table, I begin to pray,
"Thank you, God, for this new day,
for this good food, for animals, too,
And please know, God, that I love you!"

Deena Rae McClure

The animals
never yell at me

The animals never yell at me.
The animals never make me do things
I don't want to do.
They don't expect too much of me.
They don't get mean or mad.
They're always there to run with me.
And make me feel not sad.

Michael
Age 10

The new kittens

The new kittens opened their eyes today!
I wonder, God,
Are they as amazed to see me
As I am to see them?

Betty Williamson

My best friend

I have a small friend.
   Her name's Pussy Willow.
I sleep in a bed.
   She sleeps on a pillow.
When morning comes,
   and it's time to get up,
She drinks from a saucer.
   I use a cup.
I take a bath
   with my toys in a tub.
She cleans herself
   with a lick and a rub.
Her hair is quite short—
   black, orange and white.
My brown hair is long.
   I brush it each night.
She climbs up a tree.
   I go down my slide.
I skip and I hop.
   She's right by my side.

I run with my ball,
   and giggle and bounce.
She chases leaves
   with a wiggle and pounce.
She tickles my cheek
   with her soft gentle paw.
Yet she'll smack Fido's nose
   with her sharp kitty claws!
I say "I love you"
   and stroke her warm fur.
Then she squints her eyes
   and starts to purr.
She is my best friend.
   I'm never alone.
Each night I thank God
   for this cat of my own.

Jacque Hall

Frogs

Marissa likes kittens.
She's okay with dogs
but what she likes best
are little green frogs.

Marissa likes presents
like Barbies and lockets
but what she likes best
are frogs in her pockets.

Frogs in her pockets
on the way up the stairs
until her dad asks,
"What have you got there?"

God bless the children
with kittens and dogs
and bless the children
who love green frogs!

Dodie Messer Meeks

Everybody has a heart

Everybody has a heart
No matter who they are
A snake in a lake
A hog in a bog
A cat in a hat
And a frog on a log

Large or small
Short or tall
Like a little black spider
in a little green glider
and a small blue tear
on a small brown deer
Everybody has a heart
No matter who they are

Samantha Jorgensen
Age 8

Touch me

Touch me with your *voice*,
as a puppy young and new,
    And let me know my presence
    is what is pleasing you.
Touch me with your *spirit*,
for God sent me here to you,
    To teach you of that precious bond,
    known by the choicest few.
Touch me with your *hands*,
as I grow tall and strong.
    I need you as my teacher
    throughout my whole life long.
Touch me with your *lips*,
and brush them softly on my brow,
    Please kiss away the fears of life
    that I am feeling now.
Touch me with your *eyes*,
as I become full grown,
    To assure me of unspoken love,
    that we have always known.
Touch me with your *heart*,
as our bond is growing stronger,
    I pray we are together,
    forever . . . even longer.

Touch me with your *breath*,
so soft and warm upon my face,
   As I try to bring you comfort,
   in life's never-ending race.
Touch me with your *love*,
when my muzzle turns to gray,
   I have lived my life to please you,
   each and every single day.
Touch me with your *scent*,
when age has dimmed my sight,
   To reassure me always
   that you will be my light.
Touch me with your *face*,
when your tears are meant for me,
   So I may bear your pain,
   and let your heart be free.
Touch me with *remembrance*,
when I have traveled on,
   And I will hold your
   heart in mine,
   forever, when I am gone.

Susan A. Krauser

Rejoice, Animals!

PRAYERS AND POEMS OF WONDER

I am the fish

I throw myself to the left.
I turn myself to the right.
I am the fish
Who glides in the water, who glides,
Who twists himself, who leaps.
Everything lives, everything dances,
    everything sings.

Author unknown

Reptile smiles

Nothing could be grander
than a tiger salamander
when he suddenly appears
before your eyes.

Fancy little fellow
in his coat of black and yellow.
He's designed by God
to shimmer and surprise.

Carol Murray

Rejoicing

Everything is glad today
in a squeaking, piping, twittering way
all earth's creatures are having their say
with winging, singing, whispery sounds
with purring, barking, and racing around.

Patricia Lynn Spears

Morning song

It begins with a whisper
Over meadow, robin stirs.
Feathers rustle, finch and sparrow
Swift and flicker, hummer whirs.

Queedle queedle, wicka wicka
Cheer-up cheer-up, o-ka-leee.
Jay to warbler, blackbird, bunting
Sweeta sweeta, chee chee chee.

Chippa chippa, waxwing, starling
Kitter kitter, chip chip chip.
Weet weet chicka, tee-bit tweedle
Grackle, nuthatch, *kip kip kip.*

Cheep chip chippa, tuck tuck twitter
Bluebird, swallow, heed the call,
Delight this day that God has made!
Rejoice! Rejoice! One and all!

Barbara Davis-Pyles

For flying things

God gave us butterflies to dance
On rays of morning sun,
And katydids who loudly chirp
When summer days are done.
He sent the twinkling fireflies
To light the gentle night
And bumblebees with yellow coats
To kiss the flowers bright.
God created dragonflies
That dart about the sky.
Thank you, God, for all these things
That make my spirit fly.

Sandra E. McBride

29

Pigs in bliss

From our cool, damp
Piece of heaven
We grunt prayers of thanks
And wallow,
Smiling,
In muddy bliss.

Sharon Hudnell

The god of frolic

The dog was created especially for children.
He is the god of frolic.

Henry Ward Beecher
(1831–1887)

Dragonfly

This sky-ballerina
this glimmering
jewel,
glides in a gown
of lucid blue—
with wings that you
could *whisper* through.

Rebecca Kai Dotlich

Be like the bird

Be like the bird, who
Halting in his flight
On limb too slight
Feels it give way beneath him,
Yet sings
Knowing he hath wings.

Victor Hugo
(1802–1885)

Wise owl

A wise old owl sat
in an oak.
The more he heard
the less he spoke.
The less he spoke
the more he heard.
Why can't we all be like
that wise old bird?

Author unknown

Once upon
a caterpillar

Butterfly you remind me
that even if I never learn
to fly
there are many ways
to change

Arlene Gay Levine

Look at six eggs

Look at six eggs
In a mockingbird's nest.

Listen to six mockingbirds
Flinging follies of O-be-joyful
Over the marshes and uplands.

Look at songs
Hidden in eggs.

Carl Sandburg
(1878–1967)

Horses dance

Horses dance.
Tails shine under suns and moons
Strong legs move with grace
Under royal blue pink-washed
skies,
their eyes sing
gold.
Bless these wild, peaceful beasts.

Paula Timpson

If I were a blue whale

If I were a blue whale
   I would feel the salt water as blue as
the sky at night when the moon is full.

If I were a blue whale
   I would gobble the tiny krill
as small as a period.

If I were a blue whale
   I would listen to other blue whale
       mothers talking
to their babies as quietly as mice.

If I were a blue whale
  I would breathe the fresh air
as clean as a new day.

If I were a blue whale
  I would listen to the waves
      crashing against the shore
as loudly as thunder above a stormy sea.

If I were a blue whale
  I would dream of swimming to land
and walking on water.

Nicholas Spanoudis
Age 8

Be Blessed, Animals!

PRAYERS AND POEMS OF REFLECTION

The prayer of the little bird

Dear God,
I don't know how to pray by myself
very well,
but will You please
protect my little nest from wind and rain?
Put a great deal of dew on the flowers,
many seeds in my way.

Make Your blue very high,
Your branches lissome;
let Your kind light stay late in the sky
and set my heart brimming with such music
that I must sing, sing, sing . . .
Please, Lord.

                                        Amen.

Carmen Bermos de Gasztold
(translated by Rumer Godden)

In the name of St. Francis

God of All Creation,
We pray in the name of St. Francis,
Who walked the paths of
Italy many years ago.
Francis gave all that
He had to the poor,
And loved every
Creature of the earth.
Francis calmed a fierce wolf
And tamed flocks of birds
With his gentle preaching.
May we remember him today
As we love and care for all
Animals great and small.
Amen.

Barbara Younger

Little dog

Come, Little Dog, with drooping ears
And eyes that look so sad,
Come let me be the greatest pal
A puppy ever had.

I'll treat you right and feed you well;
We'll roll and jump and run,
I'll pat your head and clean your fur,
And hug you when I'm done.

And when I say my prayers at night
I'll say one for you, too,
I'll ask God while he's watching me,
To please watch over you.

Hilda Lachney Sanderson

Prayer for our stray kitten

May she nevermore be hungry;
May she find not harm nor pain.
May she always have a sheltered place
On nights of cold and rain.
May her frightened heart be settled
By my warm and loving touch.
May our soft words lightly tame her,
Then we'll spoil her (not too much!).
May we earn her trust with kindness;
May she have no cause to roam.
And may she grace for many years
These rooms that make our home.

Sharon Hudnell

The mother goose prayer

Dear God,
You protected the lamb following Mary to school
the mouse running up and down the clock
even the cow jumping over the moon.

You took care of Mother Hubbard's hungry dog
The sheep munching in the meadow
The cow trampling the corn.

You soothed Miss Muffet's spider
Rescued the blackbirds in the pie
And sent the king's horses to mend
    Humpty Dumpty.

You comforted the three little kittens who lost
    their mittens
Listened to the cat with the fiddle
Guided the pussycat to London to see the
    Fair Queen

But I have this new kitten that needs
as much help as Mother Goose's pets
Can you take care of him, too?

Donna Wahlert

Angora rabbit

Dear God, please take care of my rabbit and me.
My bunny is my funny friend
who seems to like to play pretend.
She's a gray cloud floating near the ground,
a dust-ball dancing all around,
the touch of silk against my leg,
kind, sad eyes that seem to beg
for apples, petting, hugs, or hay,
cuddly a moment, then hopping away,
a wiggly nose beneath soft fur,
a jump to my lap for me to scratch her
or thump on the grass if I'm trying to catch her.
I don't know where she's gone to hide,
But I do know You'll be at her side.

Maureen Tolman Flannery

Bless the beasts

Watch over baby animals
Who have so much to learn;
The frisky lamb out in the field,
The new calf in the barn.

The tiny kittens, weak and blind,
The naked birds in nests,
The clumsy puppy, the freckled fawn;
Dear Lord, bless all the beasts.

Shirley Nelson

A dog's prayer

Listening!
That's what I do.
Even when I sleep
I am always listening.
Give me good ears, God,
And a bark that says,
"These are my children and
I will keep them safe."
Amen.

Barbara Younger

Feather or fur

When you watch for
Feather or fur
Feather or fur
Do not stir
Do not stir.

Feather or fur
Come crawling
Creeping
Some come peeping
Some by night
And some by day.
Most come gently
All come softly
Do not scare
A friend away.

When you watch for
Feather or fur
Feather or fur
Do not stir
Do not stir.

John Becker

A prayer for my sick pet

Dear God,
I know that you love animals,
Because you filled the world
With creatures of every sort.
I love animals too,
Especially my pet
Who is sick today.
Please make my friend well
With your healing touch,
And help me to care
For the one I love.
Amen.

Barbara Younger

A good-bye prayer

Bless my friend who's gone away
I honor him this lonely day.

Lift my friend on wings of love
To Heaven lit with cheerful sun.

Dry my tears and soothe this pain
Let my world be whole again.

Kate Robinson

A pet's parting prayer

Bless this child who made my eyes
Sparkle with delight
Every time she ran to me
To hug and kiss good night.

Bless this child who made my ears
Perk to hear the sound
Of her calling me to come and play,
Or her footsteps on the ground.

Bless this child who made my nose
Wiggle with pure glee
Every time I smelled her scent
As she sat close to me.

Bless this child who made my fur
Tingle at her touch,
Or when she softly whispered,
"I love you very much."

Bless this child who made my life
A joy right to the end.
Now please find another pet
To be her special friend.

Laura Moore

When all the world's asleep

Where do insects go at night,
When all the world's asleep?
Where do bugs and butterflies
And caterpillars creep?
Turtles sleep inside their shells;
The robin has her nest.
Rabbits and the sly old fox
Have holes where they can rest.
Bears can crawl inside a cave;
The lion has his den.
Cows can sleep inside the barn,
And pigs can use their pen.
But where do bugs and butterflies
And caterpillars creep,
When everything is dark outside
And all the world's asleep?

Anita E. Posey

Please help my hamster sleep tonight

Dear Lord of awesome might
Please help my hamster sleep tonight
His running wheel goes 'round and 'round
Making that loud and squeaky sound!

Cheryl Morikawa

The white seal's lullaby

Oh! hush thee, my baby, the night is behind us,
   And black are the waters that sparkled so green.
The moon, o'er the combers, looks downward
    to find us
   At rest in the hollows that rustle between.
Where billow meets billow, there soft be thy pillow;
   Ah, weary wee flipperling, curl at thy ease!
The storm shall not wake thee, nor shark
    overtake thee,
   Asleep in the arms of the slow-swinging seas.

Rudyard Kipling
(1865–1936)

Grandpa bear's lullaby

The night is long
But fur is deep.
You will be warm
In winter sleep.

The food is gone
But dreams are sweet
And they will be
Your winter meat.

The cave is dark
But dreams are bright
And they will serve
As winter light.

Sleep, my little cubs, sleep.

Jane Yolen

Bless all living things

Dear God, protect and bless all living things.
Keep them from evil and let them sleep in peace.

Albert Schweitzer
(1875–1965)

Prayer for earth

Last night
an owl called from the hill,
coyotes howled.
A deer stood still
nibbling at bushes far away.
The moon shone silver.
Let this stay.

Today
two noisy crows
flew by
their shadows
pasted to the sky.
The sun broke out
through clouds of gray,
an iris opened.
Let this stay.

Myra Cohn Livingston

Index